BBC Gardeners' World

POCKET PLANTS

FUCHSIAS

Andi Clevely

Photographs by
Paul Bricknell and Jonathan Buckley

D0587080

BBC Books

Author Biography
Andi Clevely has been a working gardener for nearly thirty years. He began his career in Leeds City Council central nurseries and since then has worked in many gardens around the country, including Windsor Great Park. He is now responsible for a country estate and large garden in Stratford-on-Avon where he lives with his family. Andi has written a number of gardening books and is a regular columnist for *Homes & Gardens* magazine.

Acknowledgements
The publishers would like to thank Arcadia Nurseries, Middlesbrough, Teeside; C. S. Lockyer (Fuchsias), Lansbury, Bristol; Willow Tree Nurseries, Lingfield, Surrey; Askew's Nursery, Queniborough, Leicestershire; Potash Nursery, Stowmarket, Suffolk and White Veil Fuchsias, Wimborne, Dorset for their assistance with the photography. Photographs on pages 7, 9, 11, 14, 20, 34, 36, 41, 45, 48, 55, 56, 61, 68, 73 and 79 © Arcadia Nurseries.Photographs on pages 6, 8, 13, 15, 18, 19, 22, 24, 28, 29, 31, 33, 34, 35, 37, 38, 39, 42, 43, 44, 49, 50, 51, 52, 60, 64, 67, 70, 74 and 78 © BBC (Jonathan Buckley). Photographs on pages 10, 12, 16, 17, 21, 23, 25, 26, 27, 30, 32, 40, 46, 47, 53, 54, 57, 58, 59, 62, 63, 65, 66, 69, 71, 72, 75, 76, 77 and 80 © BBC (Paul Bricknell).

More Information
If you have difficulty finding any of the fushias listed in this book contact The British Fushia Society, 20 Brodawel, Llannon, Llanelli, Dyfed, SA14 6BJ.

Finding the Fuchsia for Your Garden

INTRODUCTION

Fuchsias are among the most popular flowers grown. They are widely used for annual summer bedding and hanging baskets, while the hardier kinds are planted as permanent shrubs in the flower garden; they are also supreme greenhouse pot plants.

Fuchsias are instantly recognizable, with their bright distinctive flowers in different shapes and sizes. Their colours are beguiling, both the flowers and occasionally the foliage too, for some varieties are beautifully variegated, with attractive patterns.

The choice is enormous. There are more than a hundred species, with many thousands of lovely cultivated varieties to suit every purpose.

Bedding plants

Fuchsias are widely used as summer bedding plants, grown in the open ground or in containers, as single shrubs or in small colourful groups. More vigorous specimens are sometimes planted as central 'dot' plants, often as standards.

Planting

- Fully harden plants off before planting out.

- Dig or fork the site well to ensure good drainage and add plenty of garden compost to keep the roots cool and moist. Rake in a dressing of general fertilizer just before planting.

- Water plants and stand them in position to check their arrangement and spacing.

- Using a trowel, dig a hole large enough to accommodate the rootball comfortably.

- Tap the plant from its pot, stand in position and refill the hole with the well-crumbled soil; firm in place and water thoroughly.

- Provide standards with stakes or strong canes, and tie the stems to them securely. Mulch with garden compost or grass clippings (from untreated lawns only).

Care

Water and feed regularly throughout the flowering season, and occasionally pinch out the tips of over-long shoots to encourage branching. In early autumn stop feeding, reduce watering and finally bring plants indoors when the first frost is forecast, potting them up and preparing them for winter in the same way as greenhouse specimens (see below).

Growing hardy fuchsias

A few varieties are hardy enough to grow as outdoor shrubs in most parts of the country, and there are many more that can survive the winter in milder, sheltered gardens.

Planting

- Plant in late spring in ground prepared as for bedding fuchsias.

- Dig out a hole that will take the rootball comfortably and slightly deeper, to bury the bottom 10cm (4in) of the stems and protect the lower buds from frost.

- Refill the hole with well-crumbled soil and firm in place.

- Cut down all stems to about two buds above ground level, water in thoroughly, and mulch with garden compost.

Care

Water and feed every 2–3 weeks during the first season. In the following years, water in a very dry season and feed annually in spring. In autumn, protect the roots with a mulch of leaves, bracken or straw. In mild areas the stems will survive and these are cut down in spring to 15–30cm (6–12in) above ground. Trim hedges to shape at the same time. Elsewhere old stems die right back and are cleared in spring, when plants are given a topdressing of general fertilizer.

Growing under glass

All fuchsias can be grown in a greenhouse or conservatory. Grow in a soil-based compost for good drainage, in pots ranging in size from 10cm (4in) to 20cm (8in) according to vigour.

Watering: They need regular and consistent watering, so check every day in summer. Damp down the greenhouse floor and benches in hot weather, and occasionally mist the foliage. Provide plenty of ventilation by opening vents on mild days. This prevents fungal diseases.

Feeding: Feed regularly with a high-nitrogen fertilizer in spring, changing to a high-potash formula when flower buds first appear. In most cases half-strength feeding every week for plants in soil-less composts and each fortnight for those in soil-based composts will be adequate.

Winter care: Indoor varieties need gradual drying out as the day shortens, until by mid- to late autumn pots are almost dry. Do not prune at this stage. Keep in a frost-free place, and check every few weeks that the compost is still just moist (if it is dry, soak in tepid water for an hour or two).

In late winter or early spring, cut strong shoots back to 1 or 2 buds, and remove all weak growth to leave an open shape. Repot, and stand in a warm well-lit place, but do not water until new growth appears. Water sparingly until plants are growing vigorously, after which they can be watered and trained to shape.

Training

Training is important, to create a well-balanced plant, and height and spread depend on the amount of training given. Formal shapes such as standards are grown from single cuttings, left until they reach the required height. For bushes, start training when cuttings begin growing actively or old plants produce new shoots. Cut or pinch out the growing tip of each stem just above the second or third pair of leaves (the severed tips can often be used as cuttings). Sideshoots will grow from the tops of the pruned stems, and these are pinched when they have made a similar length. Repeat several times to produce a bushy plant. Stop pinching out about 60 days before the first flowers are due.

Naming of Parts

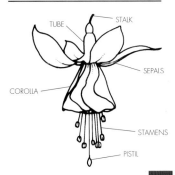

TUBE

STALK

SEPALS

COROLLA

STAMENS

PISTIL

Achievement

A very old variety that has remained popular for its strong constitution and prolific displays of bright impressive blooms. These are large, 8cm (3in) in total length, and classic both in form and colouring.

Type: Single, large-flowered.
Tube: Carmine red; medium length and thickness.
Sepals: Carmine red; long and slender, slightly upturned.
Corolla: Plum blue, becoming bright red at the base of petals.
Foliage: Large and yellowish-green, especially while still young.
Habit: Upright with strong stems, very vigorous and self-branching. Very free-flowering.
Positioning: A strong standard, ideal as a 'dot' plant in summer bedding or specimen in a pot; also for containers or outdoors. May be grown outdoors as a hardy plant In mild districts.
Care: Easy to grow. Plants are self-branching, but respond well if pinched out regularly to induce further side-shoots. Shelter from cold winds when grown outdoors and mulch well in autumn to protect the dormant roots.
Useful tips: An excellent variety for exhibition, either as a bush or standard.

Type: Single, medium-sized flowers.

Tube: Ivory white; slender.

Sepals: Ivory white tinted with rose pink, and with green tips; upturned.

Corolla: Intense rose madder with touches of white at the base of petals; neat and compact.

Foliage: Quite large, mid-green and glossy, with slightly serrated edges.

Habit: Mainly upright and very robust, freely self-branching, some of the side-shoots growing horizontally. Flowers tolerate full sun with no significant fading.

Positioning: Ideal standard for pots or a 'dot' plant for summer bedding; may be grown in containers or for bedding out.

Care: Pinch out growing tips to form bushes for bedding out after spring frosts. Bring indoors under cover in mid-autumn; as temperatures fall, monitor for mould and spray with fungicide if necessary.

Useful tips: Train as bushes or standards for late summer shows.

A charming and versatile variety, named after Liverpool's famous racecourse. The slim white buds are a particular feature, as are the brightly contrasted colours of the classically shaped blooms.

Amelie Aubin

Although this variety naturally makes a trailing plant that is perfect for hanging baskets and window-boxes, it can also be trained into more formal shapes which are effective for displaying the elegant blooms.

Type: Single, medium-sized flowers.

Tube: Clear white; long and fairly thick.

Sepals: White with green tips; dropping when first open but lifting to the horizontal as flowers mature.

Corolla: Rosy cerise, shading to white at base of petals; neat and simple.

Foliage: Large and light green, with serrated edges.

Habit: Slender willowy stems, very vigorous but needing firm support for trained forms; very free-flowering.

Positioning: Best grown in hanging baskets or at the edge of larger containers; with support may be grown as a specimen standard or pyramid in pots; can also be trained as a bush.

Care: Start into growth early and pinch out the growing tips regularly to induce the stems to branch laterally. Responds to regular full-strength feeding.

Useful tips: Worth training as a standard, which lasts several years with minimal maintenance.

Annabel

Type: Double, medium-sized flowers.

Tube: White, flushed or streaked with neyron rose; medium length and thickness.

Sepals: White tinged with rose; slightly curved away from the horizontal.

Corolla: White with subtle pink veining; very full.

Foliage: Medium-sized, light green, paler at tips.

Habit: Very vigorous upright growth, easily supporting the heavy masses of long blooms; freely self-branching. Very free-flowering.

Positioning: Ideal for bedding out in groups or as single specimens; colour develops more fully in light shade.

Care: Slightly tender, so harden off before planting out after last frosts. Feed regularly for long flowering.

Useful tips: Most effective as a bedding plant, but may also be trained as a standard, for use as a 'dot' plant in summer bedding schemes or for keeping in containers.

Almost pure white except for a hint of pink, the flowers of this outstanding variety contrast well with the pale shapely foliage. In full bloom it makes an impressive choice for summer bedding.

Ann H(oward) Tripp

Endowed with remarkable vigour, especially when young, this is a lovely variety for indoor use. With close attention to training it makes a shapely bush that is laden with masses of clean delicate blooms throughout the season.

Type:	Single or sometimes semi-double, medium-size flowers.
Tube:	White with slight pink flush; medium length and thickness.
Sepals:	White with pink edges and green tips; short and broad, held well away from the corolla.
Corolla:	Pure white with faint pink veining; small or medium in size.
Foliage:	Large and pale green; slightly yellowish when young.
Habit:	Upright, exceptionally vigorous; young plants branching freely to make dense bushes. Very prolific flowers.
Positioning:	Ideal for summer bedding although flowers are not very rain-resistant. May be grown in containers for display outdoors or under glass.
Care:	Pinch out growing tips frequently to prevent long unbranched stems. Older bushes may become bare lower down, so propagate new plants annually.
Useful tips:	Good for exhibition or display in 15–18cm (6–7in) pots.

Type:	Double, large-flowered.
Tube:	Bright red; short and quite thick.
Sepals:	Bright red; broad and recurving almost vertically along the tube.
Corolla:	White, flushed and veined with red; compact and very full.
Foliage:	Medium green, rather elongated and shapely.
Habit:	Upright and vigorous, the slim wiry stems freely branching to make a dense shapely bush. Free-flowering all season.
Positioning:	Ideal bush for a large pot indoors, or summer bedding; may be grown in a hanging basket, especially indoors.
Care:	Pinch out early and often, especially where trailing plants are required for baskets. Check for mould, and spray with fungicide if necessary.
Useful tips:	The weight of the blooms means plants must be staked securely when grown as bushes.

A bright and cheerful sight in full bloom. The flowers are very full and heavy, bending branches well down and creating the impression of a naturally trailing habit.

Autumnale

Very popular primarily as a foliage plant, although it is also a very handsome flowering variety. The stiffly spreading branches are a fascinating challenge for training into a number of highly ornamental forms. (syn. 'Rubens', 'Burning Bush'.)

Type: Single, foliage plant, medium-sized flowers.
Tube: Rosy scarlet; slender and fairly long.
Sepals: Rosy scarlet; long, slim, gracefully recurved.
Corolla: Purple; neat and compact.
Foliage: Large and variegated, yellow and green, then coppery red.
Habit: Strong-growing, with stiff branches spreading to make an open sprawling plant. Fairly free-flowering late in the season.
Positioning: Attractive in hanging baskets, containers and window-boxes; may be bedded out as a ground cover plant, or trained as a specimen pot plant.
Care: Easily grown. May be left outdoors up to first autumn frost. Overwintered plants make shapely specimens in following years, but take cuttings annually to maintain vigour.
Useful tips: Plants can be trained as very decorative standards, but are best as fans or espaliers.

Billy Green

Type:	Single, long flowers.
Tube:	Salmon pink; long and slender.
Sepals:	Salmon pink; very short and bluntly pointed.
Corolla:	Salmon pink; short and narrow.
Foliage:	Large, lush, olive green.
Habit:	Upright and vigorous, only slightly branching, making a tall shrub. Very free-flowering late in the season.
Positioning:	Sensitive to winds and low temperatures, so best grown as a pot plant in a greenhouse or conservatory, or outdoors in warm sheltered surroundings.
Care:	Never expose to hot sunshine or the cold: minimum temperature 10°C (50°F). Pot in rich compost and pinch out regularly from an early stage to avoid tall shoots. Transfer to 18–20cm (7–8in) pot by mid-summer and feed fortnightly throughout flowering. Bring plants indoors before the autumn frosts.
Useful tips:	Trains quickly as a large standard.

Possibly the most vigorous of the many lovely *triphylla* hybrids, this will make a tall strong bush, or with care can be trained from a cutting into a flowering standard in one year. Very dramatic and almost tropical in appearance when in full bloom.

A fine all-rounder, very obliging and easy to grow, producing its heavy crops of large, well-shaped blooms from early in the season. One of the best for general use, especially for bedding out in the garden in summer.

Type:	Single or sometimes semi-double, large-flowered.
Tube:	Greenish-white; short and thick.
Sepals:	Clean white with green tips; reflexed.
Corolla:	Rich magenta, slightly darker along the edges and white at the base.
Foliage:	Fairly large, light or mid-green, with serrated edges.
Habit:	Vigorous growth, upright then rather spreading, especially when weighed down with blooms. Early and very prolific flowers.
Positioning:	Excellent in summer bedding or as a specimen in mixed borders; also grows well under glass as a bush or semi-trailer.
Care:	Trouble free. Pinch occasionally to develop strong, wide bushes, more often for semi-trailers. Feed regularly during the flowering season. Bring plants inside in early autumn to avoid mould.
Useful tips:	Plants can be shaped as specimen pot plants indoors with support.

❋❋ **◉**

Type:	Single, medium-sized flowers.
Tube:	Cherry red; short and rounded.
Sepals:	Cherry red; curving gracefully upwards.
Corolla:	Deep purple, shading to carmine at the base and ageing to reddish-purple.
Foliage:	Medium-sized, mid-green with red veins, almost horizontal.
Habit:	Very vigorous and upright, the fairly stiff stems branching freely to make a bushy plant. Free-flowering over a long season.
Positioning:	At home indoors or in summer bedding; may be trained into upright shapes.
Care:	Easily pleased and able to cope with dry difficult conditions indoors or out. Feed and water regularly for magnificent specimens, that can be overwintered in the cool for reviving into growth early the following year.
Useful tips:	Excellent for training in large pots as pyramids or cones.

A classic red and purple variety, almost a century old, with prolific blooms of good substance and neat shape. Plants tolerate a wide range of conditions, making very large bushes that start flowering early.

Cascade

As its name implies, this is an outstanding trailing variety for hanging baskets and other aerial containers, and also for large containers where its blooms can hang clear in luxuriant trusses. Even the long, elegantly curved buds are attractive.

Type:	Single, large-flowered.
Tube:	White, flushed with carmine; thin and medium in length.
Sepals:	White, flushed or fringed with carmine; long, slim and pointing downwards with a slight reflex.
Corolla:	Deep rose bengal, sometimes white-tinged at the base of the petals.
Foliage:	Medium-sized, light or mid-green and finely serrated.
Habit:	Very vigorous and self-branching, with lax flexible branches that soon trail downwards. Very free-flowering over a long season.
Positioning:	Superb for containers that will keep the branches clear of the ground.
Care:	Pinch out once or twice before plants branch naturally. Plant early in hanging baskets and suspend in a greenhouse until it is warm enough to move them outdoors.
Useful tips:	A good choice for an urn or jardinière; try 2–3 plants in a tub.

Type: Single, medium-sized flowers.

Tube: Greenish-white, sometimes tinged with pink; medium length and thickness.

Sepals: Pinkish-white, underside darker and almost rose; gently and smoothly upturned.

Corolla: Vivid redcurrant red, with a white flare at the base of each petal; neat and shapely.

Foliage: Large, pale or mid-green with red veins.

Habit: Very vigorous, strong and upright, the erect stems making a tall and fairly well-branched bush. Very free-flowering

Positioning: Ideal as a standard, but also makes a good pot plant and may be bedded out in summer, in full sun or light shade.

Care: Easy to grow, but pinch out carefully and often at an early stage to produce a bushy plant.

Useful tips: Strong cuttings can be grown into attractive standards in a single season.

One of the best varieties for ease of cultivation and all-round adaptability. Very popular because of the unusual colour of its corolla, a clear and vivid shade of red that does not turn blue as it ages and does not fade in sunlight.

Chang

A hybrid of *Fuchsia cordifolia*, with a habit less uniform and predictable than more highly bred varieties, and plants seem determined to resist efforts to train them into formal shapes. But even when left to grow naturally, their profuse flowers are always radiant and eye-catching.

Type: Single, small-flowered.

Tube: Orange-red; long in proportion to the rest of the flower, and quite thick.

Sepals: Pale orange-red, the underside much lighter, with green tips; tightly curving upwards.

Corolla: Rich brilliant orange; short, slightly flared.

Foliage: Medium-sized, sometimes quite large, mid-green.

Habit: Vigorous and upright, with strong stems that need careful training to produce a leafy bush. Very profuse flowers, especially outdoors.

Positioning: Excellent for bedding out in summer, when it will flower more freely; makes a tall subject for formal training. Best planted in full sun.

Care: Easy to grow if allowed to go its own way. Pinch out frequently from an early stage for trained forms.

Useful tips: With frequent tying and training, a strong cutting can be grown into a tall arching standard in a season or so.

Type: Single, medium-sized flowers.

Tube: Light red, or white tinged with red; long and slender.

Sepals: White, rose red at base; slightly reflexed.

Corolla: Rose red, paler at the base of the petals; tight and compact.

Foliage: Medium-sized, mid- to dark green, serrated.

Habit: Very strong growth, with vigorous long-jointed stems that produce a large open bush. Early and prolific flowers.

Positioning: Ideal for bedding out in summer and for growing in pots indoors or in larger planting schemes in outdoor containers; makes a decorative tall fan against a wall.

Care: Revive plants into growth in late winter and trim to shape before growth is too vigorous, so that flowers can develop in time for early displays.

Useful tips: A strong cutting soon makes a tall standard, but train carefully to avoid producing a stiff top-heavy plant.

Dainty and distinctive, with two-coloured flowers that match its name. Robust and early flowering, it is an asset in any collection, but do not try to train plants too tightly because the habit is naturally very open and airy.

Slightly more demanding than most varieties, but well worth the extra care, and very rewarding when it produces its masses of unusually graceful blooms with their swirling bell-shaped skirts.

Type: Single, medium-sized flowers.

Tube: Light red or rosy pink; short and fairly thick.

Sepals: Light red; turned upwards to touch the tube.

Corolla: White with clear pink veins at the base; widely flared when blooms are fully open.

Foliage: Medium-sized, light or mid-green, developing red veins with age.

Habit: Upright and very vigorous, forming a shapely bushy plant. Very free-flowering.

Positioning: Grow in pots and larger containers, both outdoors in summer and under glass; also good for bedding in a semi-shaded position.

Care: Susceptible to mould, so take care with watering and ventilation under glass, and spray if necessary with fungicide. Feed regularly to sustain flowering and prevent early leaf drop.

Useful tips: For the best colouring grow outdoor plants in some shade, and under glass shield them from bright sunlight.

Cliff's Hardy

Type: Single, medium-sized flowers.

Tube: Crimson; medium length and thickness.

Sepals: Crimson with green tips; long, slender and gently recurving.

Corolla: Violet-blue, fading slightly at the base and with clear scarlet veins; neatly flared.

Foliage: Small or medium-sized, mid-dark green.

Habit: Vigorous and upright growth, the stems branching freely to form naturally compact bushy plants. Very free-flowering.

Positioning: Grow in pots under cool glass or in containers outdoors; may also be bedded out in summer. In many areas it is hardy or semi-hardy and can be planted permanently outdoors in a warm sheltered spot.

Care: Water in dry weather and feed regularly. Mulch outdoor plants in autumn to protect roots against frost.

Useful tips: Plant 30cm (12in) apart for a compact hedge, 45–75cm (18–30in) high.

With plenty of healthy foliage and classic flowers that are held upright and well out from the stems, this is a reliable variety that makes good-looking plants indoors and out.

This is grown more for its sunny yellow foliage than for its blooms, which appear later than normal flowering varieties. Nonetheless, the flowers are richly coloured and charming, even in bud when they resemble fat, slightly pointed balls.

Type: Single, small-flowered.

Tube: Red; short and thick.

Sepals: Red; broad and bluntly pointed, horizontal or arching downwards.

Corolla: Purple; short and compact.

Foliage: Strong golden-yellow ageing to green with a bronze flush, reddish underneath.

Habit: Upright growth at first then almost horizontal; self-branching, making an open plant. Moderately free-flowering, from fairly late in the season.

Positioning: Good for summer bedding, in full sun at the front of a border; also a good pot plant.

Care: Start into growth as early as possible to make maximum size before planting out. Grow in good light at all times and avoid over-watering. Plant out after the last frosts and rehouse before the first frosts.

Useful tips: Dryish conditions intensify the foliage colours, so only water as necessary. Grow pot plants in free-draining soil-based compost.

Coachman

Type: Single, medium-sized flowers.

Tube: Light salmon pink; short and thick.

Sepals: Light salmon pink with green tips; broad and held stiffly just below the horizontal.

Corolla: Orange vermilion; short and compact.

Foliage: Large, rich green and matt.

Habit: Strong vigorous growth upright, then almost pendent. Self-branching, producing a fine bushy plant. Very free-flowering, starting early but with short pauses.

Positioning: Train as a standard for pots or 'dot' plant in summer bedding. Stems can also be trained for hanging baskets and window-boxes.

Care: Very easy to grow and totally trouble free. Pinch out regularly to stimulate horizontal branching for growing in baskets.

Useful tips: Overwinters easily, eventually making large plants that become impressive as they age.

An old variety introduced early this century, this is still popular for its fine colouring and adaptability. The strong but flexible growth makes excellent large standards, and also very bushy plants suitable for hanging baskets.

23

Coralle

One of the best known and most widely available hybrids, with a good strong constitution if given plenty of warmth. Even quite small plants produce their large bunches of slim flowers, 5cm (2in) long, over a generous season. (syn. 'Koralle'.)

Type:	Single, long flowers.
Tube:	Coral red; very long, medium thickness.
Sepals:	Coral red; short and bluntly pointed.
Corolla:	Coral red; small and compact.
Foliage:	Medium to large, deep sage green with paler veins and an overall velvety sheen.
Habit:	Very strong upright stems that respond well to pinching out by producing dense bushy growth. Very free-flowering.
Positioning:	Very sensitive to cold; grow as a pot plant in the greenhouse or conservatory, or outside in summer in a warm, sheltered place.
Care:	Withstands full sunlight but not the cold, so harden off and stand outdoors in early summer. Pot in rich compost and pinch out regularly for broad bushy plants.. Water and feed regularly during flowering, and rehouse before autumn frosts. Overwinter at 10°C (50°F).
Useful tips:	Best as a simple bush. Ideal for exhibition.

Type: Single, small or medium-sized flowers.

Tube: Creamy white; short and thick.

Sepals: White, sometimes tinged with pink; upturned, often touching the tube.

Corolla: Creamy white with a slight pink tinge; small.

Foliage: Small to medium-sized, mid-green.

Habit: Quite strong upright growth, self-branching to produce a dense short-jointed bush. Free-flowering.

Positioning: Grow as a bush, in pots indoors or out; may also be bedded out after the last frosts; for the best colouring, plant or stand in some shade with shelter from winds.

Care: Keep the foliage fairly dry to guard against mould. Keep training to a minimum. Propagate in spring from short tips only, as hardwood cuttings at other times are often slow to root.

Useful tips: Grow as short or medium standards but do not pinch out growing tips too often.

A very old nineteenth-century variety, famous for its enchanting delicate colouring, but equally notorious for being rather fussy. When well grown, plants have a charming and aristocratic appearance.

Dollar Princess

A very well-known variety that excels in most forms, especially outdoors where it is reliably hardy in many gardens. Although small, the perfectly shaped flowers appear continuously in great masses, often covering the branches. (syn. 'Princess Dollar'.)

❋❋	🔥

Type: Double, small-flowered.

Tube: Cerise; small and medium thickness.

Sepals: Cerise; fairly broad and reflexing almost to touch the tube.

Corolla: Deep purple, with cerise markings at the base of petals; small.

Foliage: Small to medium-sized, mid- or deep green and serrated.

Habit: Very vigorous upright growth, self-branching freely to make a compact bushy plant. Flowers prolifically.

Positioning: Best as a bush, in outdoor containers or as summer bedding; may be planted permanently outside in a warm sheltered place. Easily trained as a standard for indoors or a 'dot' plant outside.

Care: Pinch out only once or twice for bushy growth. Feed outdoor plants regularly and mulch for winter with autumn leaves; do not prune old stems until spring.

Useful tips: Plant 38–45cm (15–18in) apart for a summer hedge.

Empress of Prussia

Type: Single, medium to large-flowered.

Tube: Scarlet; short and thick.

Sepals: Scarlet; broad and compact, slightly above horizontal.

Corolla: Magenta to scarlet, paler at the base; short and widely flared.

Foliage: Medium-sized and broad, mid- or deep green, slightly serrated.

Habit: Very sturdy upright growth, with thick stems that branch freely to produce a dense bush. Free-flowering.

Positioning: Ideal for permanent outdoor cultivation, as a specimen or in small groups; also succeeds as a large container plant, both outside and under cool glass.

Care: Plant out in spring, then feed regularly for strong growth. Protect in winter with a mulch of leaves and do not prune until the spring. In the second year continue feeding every fortnight; from then on an annual spring mulch of garden compost will be sufficient.

Useful tips: A good choice for a strong standard.

Outstanding as a hardy fuchsia, this very old variety was lost for many years and only recently reintroduced. The blooms are large for a hardy type and very prolific, with six to eight flowers at each leaf joint instead of the more normal pair.

Eva Boerg

A great favourite when trailing from a hanging basket, the flowers of this variety are carried on long, gracefully arching stems. Equally at home in a container indoors and planted outside as a garden shrub.

Type: Single or semi-double, medium-sized flowers.

Tube: Greenish-white; short and thick.

Sepals: White, flushed pink and with green tips; broad and reflexed.

Corolla: Light purple, splashed with pink and paler at the base of petals; fairly loose.

Foliage: Medium-sized, pale to mid-green, oval and serrated.

Habit: Hardy and vigorous, with stems upright at first but tending to arch under the weight of the blooms. Very free-flowering all season.

Positioning: May be grown for hanging baskets, as a bush for containers or for bedding out in summer; also as a permanent border shrub.

Care: Very easy. Laden stems may benefit from support. Mulch outdoor plants with leaves in autumn, and feed occasionally in summer; prune old stems down in spring.

Useful tips: Try planting 30–38cm (12–15in) apart for an informal hedge.

Type: Single, medium-sized flowers.

Tube: White; long and slender.

Sepals: White with green tips; long, slim and completely recurving to the tube, with a slight twist.

Corolla: Rich blue at first, maturing to reddish-purple, with white markings at the base of petals.

Foliage: Medium-sized, mid-green, finely serrated.

Habit: Vigorous and strong-growing, with long stems that are upright at first but later become fairly lax. Exceptionally free-flowering.

Positioning: Best in large pots or bedded outdoors in shelter for summer.

Care: Pinch out tips regularly to induce branching – early for good bushes or when standards reach their full height. The foliage is prone to mould, so aim for an open structure and spray with fungicide at the first signs of trouble.

Useful tips: Plants need room to look their best.

A well-grown specimen is breathtaking, both for its graceful shape and for the elegance of its radiant blooms. These open almost in slow motion, the shining sepals gradually extending over 2–3 days to frame the corolla like a beautifully lit lantern.

Frosted Flame

As its name suggests, this variety is outstanding for the dramatic and contrasting colouring of its flowers. These start early in the season, in such great numbers that the foliage is often hidden from sight, and a mature specimen in a hanging basket is a memorable sight.

Type: Single, medium to large flowers.

Tube: Waxy white; medium length and thickness.

Sepals: White outside and pale pink within, with green tips; long, slender, held well out.

Corolla: Bright flame red, with deeper edges, fading to pink near the tube; barrel shaped with overlapping petals.

Foliage: Medium to large, bright green.

Habit: Vigorous naturally trailing stems branching freely to produce a bushy plant. Very free-flowering over a long season.

Positioning: Perfect for hanging baskets and window-boxes; also for trailing over a low wall or the edge of a tub. Grow in light shade for the best colouring.

Care: Start into growth in late winter and pinch several times to make a good-sized bush before early flowers appear. Feed every fortnight to sustain the display.

Useful tips: Train on canes as a fan in a large pot.

Gartenmeister Bonstedt

Type: Single, very long triphylla flowers.

Tube: Brick red; long and slightly bulging.

Sepals: Brick red; small and bluntly pointed.

Corolla: Brick red; short and compact.

Foliage: Medium to large, dark bronze-green and reddish beneath.

Habit: Extremely vigorous, with strong upright, slow-branching stems. Plants are sturdy and make tall specimens. Very free-flowering over a long season.

Positioning: Best grown as a bush, in pots and containers indoors or out, or bedded as a half-hardy plant outdoors.

Care: Pinch out several times for a good bush. Never expose to low temperatures and move outdoors well after spring frosts. Bring inside in early autumn and overwinter in a minimum temperature of 10°C (50°F).

Useful tips: Cuttings root readily and quickly make tall single stems if not stopped. Not easily trained as a standard.

Named after one of the great hybridizers and almost the oldest *triphylla* variety. A favourite choice for pot cultivation, although it also performs well outdoors in a warm position, flowering consistently over the whole season.

Golden Marinka

One or two specimens of this richly coloured variety, planted in a hanging basket in full sun, will produce a glowing mass of golden foliage that would be stunning even without the bonus of its blooms. The coloured counterpart of green-leafed 'Marinka', equally popular for planting in baskets.

Type: Single, medium-sized flowers.

Tube: Dark red; long with medium thickness.

Sepals: Dark red; short and broad, held right over the corolla.

Corolla: Slightly deeper red; neat and compact.

Foliage: Medium-sized, green variegated with golden-yellow margins and red veins.

Habit: Fairly vigorous, with strong stems that grow stiffly in a horizontal position unless supported. Flowers fairly late in the season.

Positioning: Hanging baskets and other containers. Best grown in full sun for the richest colouring.

Care: Avoid over-watering as mould can be a problem – err on the dry side, and spray with fungicide if symptoms appear. Pinch to encourage early branching. Overwinter at about 10°C (50°F).

Useful tips: Train as standards with firm support and tying in at the early stages.

Type: Double, small to medium-sized flowers.

Tube: Crimson; short and thick.

Sepals: Crimson-cerise; broad, short and reflexed.

Corolla: Bright lilac, veined with red and paler at the base of the petals; very fluffy and filled with extra small petals.

Foliage: Small, dark green with red midribs and finely serrated.

Habit: Vigorous and upright, a compact bushy plant with plenty of small foliage. Flowers early and continues throughout the season.

Positioning: An excellent small pot plant indoors or in a conservatory; may also be planted outside as a half-hardy bedding variety. Train as a short standard for indoor pot cultivation.

Care: Start into growth in late winter. Pinch once or twice to stimulate plenty of side-shoots and feed regularly.

Useful tips: 'White Ann' is a red and white sport of this variety, with similar growth and as good for indoor display.

Some fuchsia varieties are particularly suited to indoor display in pots, and this lovely compact plant is one of them, although its unusual fluffy double blooms are perfectly weatherproof for outdoor cultivation as well.

Impudence

This is highly popular for its brightly coloured and unusual blooms. The corolla is composed of four almost circular petals that overlap and fan out to make a flat and airy skirt. A remarkable sight in full bloom.

Type: Single, medium-sized flowers.

Tube: Carmine red; short with medium thickness.

Sepals: Carmine red; broad and recurving upwards to the tube.

Corolla: White with carmine veining; petals spread out horizontally and widely flared.

Foliage: Medium-sized, mid-green and serrated.

Habit: Very strong-growing with tall upright stems and well-spaced leaf joints. Very free-flowering from early in the season.

Positioning: Best grown as a pot plant indoors or in containers outside; may also be bedded out in summer, and can be shaped into an attractive fan.

Care: Start plants into growth early and pinch regularly to train them into shape. Feed regularly to maintain the long display.

Useful tips: The long sturdy stems can produce a good fan or espalier if pinched early in life to stimulate plenty of side-shoots.

Type:	Double, medium-sized flowers.
Tube:	Scarlet; medium length and thickness.
Sepals:	Very bright scarlet; long, slim and recurving.
Corolla:	Royal blue; very full and slightly loose.
Foliage:	Medium-sized, dark green.
Habit:	Strong-growing, with long branches that soon arch down in a trailing position. Free-flowering.
Positioning:	Mainly grown in hanging baskets, window-boxes and other containers. With careful training plants may also be grown in pots indoors or bedded out in summer with some support.
Care:	Totally trouble free. Pinch hard several times while still small to produce well-branched bushes. Feed regularly for heavy flowering.
Useful tips:	Plants can be trained as fans if they are pinched early to make strong radiating shoots.

This is noted for its elegance and the splendour of its vivid blooms. The colours remain radiant all season with no serious fading in bright light, while their quantity and continuity are exceptional. A lovely variety in every respect.

A handsome variety with a satisfyingly dense habit and elegant flowers that deserve prominent display. The corolla of each bloom is widely flared, giving flowering plants the appearance of being decorated with small open parasols.

Type: Single, medium-sized flowers.

Tube: Light magenta with darker veins; short with medium thickness.

Sepals: Light pink with crêped underside; broad, pointed and slightly reflexed.

Corolla: Rose magenta with a metallic lustre; short and flared.

Foliage: Medium-sized, rich green, slightly serrated.

Habit: Very vigorous growth, self-branching freely to make dense compact bushes. Very free-flowering throughout the season.

Positioning: Ideal for growing in a pot indoors or in decorative containers outside in summer. Stands out best in a lightly shaded position.

Care: Easy to grow. Avoid wetting the prolific foliage as a precaution against mould, and feed regularly throughout the season.

Useful tips: Effective when grown as a standard, but support well when training the short-jointed growth as a straight main stem.

Type: Single, medium-sized flowers.

Tube: Bengal pink; long with medium thickness.

Sepals: Bengal pink with green tips; long, slim and almost horizontal.

Corolla: Rose pink; neatly overlapping.

Foliage: Medium-sized, mid-green, fairly long and serrated.

Habit: Vigorous and strong-growing, producing stems that are almost horizontal, and freely self-branching into a naturally trailing bush. Very free-flowering.

Positioning: Excellent for hanging baskets, especially in light shade, but equally successful in urns and window-boxes; may also be trained as a standard.

Care: No special care needed. Regular pinching to stimulate as many side-shoots as possible will help to produce a more even display of flowers.

Useful tips: Plants make impressive weeping standards for growing in pots or in a summer bedding scheme.

Well known and widely recommended for growing in hanging baskets. It is also outstanding for window-box cultivation, its long self-branching stems holding the richly coloured blooms well clear of the container.

Joy Patmore

Growth is more restrained than for most other varieties, and bushes remain small and manageable, especially in pots. As a standard, though, this variety is outstanding, making a dense head that is covered with distinctive, striking flowers.

Type: Single, medium-sized flowers.

Tube: White; short and thick.

Sepals: Waxy white; slender and reflexing.

Corolla: Bright carmine red, slightly darker at the edges and fading to white at the base of petals; opens to a full bell.

Foliage: Medium-sized, mid-green.

Habit: Moderately vigorous, branching freely to produce a bushy, medium-sized plant of compact shape, Very free-flowering.

Positioning: Ideal for pots indoors or out; may be bedded out in summer at the front of beds and borders. Trained as standards, plants are successful in pots or outdoors as 'dot' plants for summer bedding.

Care: Very easy to grow and train. Pinch while still young to induce further branching, and feed regularly throughout the flowering season.

Useful tips: Plants gradually grow into mature bushes with even more spectacular displays of flowers.

La Campanella

Type: Semi-double, small to medium-sized flowers.

Tube: White, faintly tinged with pink; short and thick.

Sepals: White above, flushed pink on the underside; broad and fairly short, with tips turning upwards at first and then fully reflexing.

Corolla: Purple ageing to lavender, with slight cerise veining.

Foliage: Small, medium green.

Habit: Very vigorous growth, eventually trailing, but also makes a dense bush. Very free-flowering all season.

Positioning: Suitable for outdoor hanging baskets; can also be trained on a strong cane as a standard in containers or a 'dot' plant among summer bedding.

Care: No special requirements, and not susceptible to pests or diseases. Responds well to early pinching and supplementary feeding.

Useful tips: Readily propagated from cuttings; also sets plenty of good seeds.

A well-known and popular variety for its overall outstanding qualities of vigour, good health and rapid growth, and one that is ideal for beginners to train into various forms.

Lady Isobel Barnett

Fine and flamboyant, arguably one of the most free-flowering varieties ever raised. The widely open blooms are held out firmly on strong stalks and face confidently outwards or even slightly upwards in a spectacular and continuous display.

Type: Single, medium-sized flowers.

Tube: Rose red; medium length and fairly thick.

Sepals: Rose red; held straight out.

Corolla: Pink and lavender with royal purple edges; very open.

Foliage: Medium-sized, light to mid-green, serrated.

Habit: Very vigorous and robust, with strong tall, upright and freely self-branching stems. Exceptionally free-flowering all season.

Positioning: A strong bush for large containers, indoors or in light shade; may be bedded out as a bold summer shrub. Can be trained as a pillar or espalier in a large pot under glass or against a warm sheltered wall.

Care: Trouble free. Needs regular training because growth is so vigorous. Pinch frequently while small, and feed regularly during training.

Useful tips: Pollen may disfigure the leaves unless they are wiped.

Type: Single, medium-sized flowers.

Tube: Creamy white, often with a hint of pink; medium length.

Sepals: Creamy white outside and rosy pink beneath, green tips; slender, long, well presented.

Corolla: Lavender blue, veined with pale pink.

Foliage: Medium-sized, mid-green, soft and tender.

Habit: Moderately vigorous upright stems that are flexible and later quite lax. Fairly free-flowering.

Positioning: Best grown as a bush, indoors or as a half-hardy bedding plant. Grow in shade to protect colours, and shelter from winds.

Care: Pinch young plants and feed regularly during training. Inspect for greenfly and red spider mite. Take cuttings in autumn, and monitor for mould.

Useful tips: For an unusual trailing plant – pinch hard while small, then weight or tie down the lateral branches to stimulate horizontal growth.

The softly coloured blooms of this attractive variety have a calm elegance that is particularly satisfying in light shade. Although the foliage is susceptible to pests and diseases, this is a lovely variety when grown well.

Lena

Among the oldest varieties still widely cultivated, and certainly one of the easiest to grow well. Plants are obliging and versatile, responding to training into most forms, while the flowers appear continuously in huge and impressive quantities.

Type: Single or semi-double, medium-sized flowers.

Tube: Cream/flesh pink; short and fairly thick.

Sepals: Pale flesh pink with darker undersides and green tips; broad and upturned.

Corolla: Purple, turning crimson as flowers fade, and pink at the base of the petals.

Foliage: Medium-sized, light to mid-green, serrated.

Habit: Vigorous and self-branching, producing a neat compact bush with arching growth. Very free-flowering.

Positioning: Easily trained, either as a bush for indoor pots, or permanently outside in a lightly shaded bed or border (colours may fade badly in strong light). Can also be bedded out for the summer. Can be adapted for basket cultivation, or trained as a small standard.

Care: Totally trouble free. Pinch out plants while still young to stimulate bushy growth.

Useful tips: Withstands warm dry conditions so makes an ideal house plant.

Type:	Single, medium-sized flowers.
Tube:	Clear pink; medium length and fairly thick.
Sepals:	Clear pink with green tips; long, slim and recurving.
Corolla:	Pink, tinged and veined lightly with lilac; bell-shaped.
Foliage:	Small or medium-sized, mid-green and serrated.
Habit:	Vigorous, with strong uniform growth making a compact and evenly balanced bush. Very free-flowering, continuing well into the autumn.
Positioning:	Excellent for pots or as a bedding plant in summer – always grow cool in light shade to preserve the delicate colouring. Also trains easily as a standard.
Care:	Completely trouble free. Pinch young plants to stimulate self-branching, and feed regularly during training.
Useful tips:	Stand pots outdoors in light shade in summer, moving them into stronger light in early autumn.

Widely recommended as a natural and easily grown bush variety, although it is also ideal for training as a standard: this is perhaps the most impressive way to display its sparkling blooms, which are among the best of any self-pink fuchsia.

A lovely trailing variety that is charming in its imperfection, almost as though the slightly loose growth might be a necessary balance to the artless grace of its large, slender-stalked pink and white blooms.

Type: Double, large-flowered.

Tube: White with a pink flush; long and fairly thick.

Sepals: White above, frosted white flushed with light pink beneath; long, slender and reflexed, sometimes twisted.

Corolla: Shades of rose pink, with darker veining; long and compact.

Foliage: Medium-sized, rich green and serrated, in dense masses.

Habit: Vigorous stems, often twisting as they cascade downwards. Very free-flowering.

Positioning: Good for hanging baskets, especially in light shade where the colours are more prominent; also effective cascading over the edge of a tub, or trailing over a bank or low wall.

Care: Pinch young plants to ensure bushy plants. Feed during training. Plant up in a large basket as the root system can become quite extensive.

Useful tips: Train as fans, pillars and espaliers.

Type: Single, medium-sized flowers.

Tube: Rose red; medium length and fairly thick.

Sepals: Rose red; short, broad and reflexed almost upright against the tube.

Corolla: Rosy lilac, pale red at the base of the petals and veined with red; opens almost flat.

Foliage: Small to medium-sized, mid-green with red veins and stems, long and serrated.

Habit: Upright growth of moderate vigour, branching freely. Very free-flowering.

Positioning: Best grown as a bush, in pots under glass or grouped in larger containers outdoors in summer; may be bedded out in shade.

Care: Pinch to encourage young plants to branch low down, and feed regularly. Overwinter annually to develop large bushes.

Useful tips: Standards, which are easily trained as container plants or 'dot' plants in sheltered spots, display the flowers well.

The result of crossing 'Impudence' with 'Joy Patmore', hence the fairly restrained growth habit and also the arresting flower structure – the corolla opens out quite flat above an open and prominent cluster of stamens, adding lightness and grace to the plants.

Lye's Unique

An old and well-loved variety, equally valuable as a strong bush or well-branched standard, and one of the best introductions by the famous nineteenth-century hybridizer James Lye. A plant of exceptional beauty.

Type: Single, medium-sized flowers.

Tube: Waxy, white; long, thick and very firm.

Sepals: Waxy, ivory white; narrow, held almost horizontally.

Corolla: Salmon-orange; neat and compact.

Foliage: Medium-sized, dull, dark green.

Habit: Strong upright growth, very vigorous and freely self-branching. Very free-flowering.

Positioning: Can be grown in large pots indoors or in containers outside during summer; also plant out as a specimen shrub during summer. Very successful as a tall standard in a pot or as a 'dot' plant among summer bedding.

Care: Trouble free. The firm stems make good long cuttings for standards; bushes are best grown from soft tip cuttings pinched out at an early stage.

Useful tips: Side-shoots are easily trained outwards to develop attractive pyramids and espaliers for pot cultivation.

Madame Cornelissen

Type: Single to semi-double, smallish flowers.

Tube: Rich crimson; short, medium thickness.

Sepals: Rich crimson; held almost horizontally.

Corolla: White with cerise veining; fairly compact.

Foliage: Small longish leaves, dark green, serrated.

Habit: Moderately vigorous and stiffly upright, with a distinctive spiky appearance. Free-flowering.

Positioning: Usually grown for pot cultivation indoors or outside in summer; also suitable for bedding out singly or in small groups. Very hardy and ideal for growing permanently in a warm position.

Care: Undemanding. Water outdoor plants in a dry season and feed container plants regularly. Little training is necessary after one or two early pinchings.

Useful tips: Try growing a group of three 45cm (18in) apart, to merge as a single bold shrub.

A fine hardy fuchsia with a distinctive upright habit that needs little training. Equally popular for indoor and garden cultivation, its lasting attraction is the vivid colour scheme of its beautiful and long-lasting flowers.

Effective summer bedding depends on bright, eye-catching colours and free-flowering continuity, qualities this cheerful variety has in good measure. The flowers have remarkably dense colouring and in full sunlight appear to sparkle brilliantly.

Type: Single, small flowered.

Tube: Orange-red; thin, medium thickness.

Sepals: Orange-red with green tips; short, narrow and held well out from the corolla.

Corolla: Deep brick red; neat and compact.

Foliage: Small to medium-sized, medium green and serrated.

Habit: Moderately vigorous with strong upright stems that branch freely. Free-flowering.

Positioning: Makes neat uniform bushes for bedding out in summer in full sun or light shade; makes a good container plant outdoors. May be trained as a short (quarter) standard.

Care: Pinch out plants while still small to induce free self-branching. Feed regularly and keep consistently moist at all times, but avoid over-watering.

Useful tips: Plants tend to shed buds and flowers in dry conditions, so this is unsuitable for use as an exhibition variety or for growing indoors as a pot plant.

Margaret

Type: Semi-double, small flowered.

Tube: Scarlet or carmine; medium length and thickness.

Sepals: Scarlet or carmine; reflexed over the tube.

Corolla: Violet-purple, pink at the base of the petals, with cerise veining; very full.

Foliage: Small to medium-sized, mid-green and shiny.

Habit: Vigorous and upright, with robust stems freely self-branching. Very free-flowering.

Positioning: Best grown outdoors only, in a bed, where it will develop into a large bush in 2 years.

Care: Plant in late spring and feed every 2 weeks with half-strength fertilizer during the first season. Protect in the first winter and leave top growth unpruned until the young stems start growing in the spring. In the second season feed fortnightly at full strength.

Useful tips: If planted 45-60cm (18-24in) apart, bushes make a hedge about 1.2-1.4m (4-4½ft) high.

A tough plant and one of the best red/purple varieties for outdoor cultivation. Although the individual blooms are fairly small, they are produced in great numbers, so that bushes make a brilliant and eye-catching display all season.

Mission Bells

A popular and prolific variety, with flowers in the typical red and purple fuchsia combination. The blooms change quite noticeably as they mature, however, the formerly neat purple corolla flaring to a wide bell shape and changing colour to plum red.

Type: Single, medium-sized flowers.

Tube: Scarlet; short, medium thickness.

Sepals: Scarlet and shiny; medium length, broad and reflexing.

Corolla: Vivid purple, shading to red at base of the petals; bell shaped.

Foliage: Medium-sized, dull mid-green and serrated.

Habit: Vigorous and strong-growing with stems that are stiffly upright at first then droop under the weight of blooms. Free-flowering, although sometimes late to start.

Positioning: Useful as half-hardy bedding plants in summer; excellent in pots in the conservatory and for containers outdoors. May also be trained as a standard. Best in light shade.

Care: Young plants need frequent pinching to encourage low branching.

Useful tips: As trained plants age their wood becomes brittle; old standards, for example, should be planted in sheltered spots.

Mrs Popple

Type: Single, medium-sized flowers.

Tube: Scarlet; short and thin.

Sepals: Scarlet; short and broad.

Corolla: Violet-purple, paler at base of petals and lightly veined with cerise; neatly furled.

Foliage: Small, dark green, narrow and serrated.

Habit: Vigorous and bushy, with strong upright growth that becomes slightly trailing. Free-flowering.

Positioning: Normally grown as a hardy garden variety, individually or in groups; may be grown as a pot plant, in bush form or as a standard, under glass or outdoors.

Care: Permanent outdoor plants should be fed regularly during the first two seasons while they develop into full-size bushes; protect during the first winter, and prune the dead stems in spring.

Useful tips: Plants may be spaced 45–60cm (18–24in) apart to make a hedge up to 1.2m (4ft) high.

One of the best-known and best-loved hardy varieties for general garden use and also for ornamental hedges. The brilliant and prolific flowers are quite large for a hardy fuchsia, 5–6cm (2–2½in) long, and produced over a long season.

Mrs W Rundle

Renowned for over a century and still widely regarded as a fine variety of subtle loveliness. The long blooms hang in crowded bunches at the ends of elegantly drooping branches, giving plants an almost weeping appearance.

Type: Single, medium-sized flowers.

Tube: Flesh pink; long and slender.

Sepals: Flesh pink with green tips; long, narrow and slightly reflexing.

Corolla: Orange crimson; compact and tightly furled.

Foliage: Medium-sized, light green, broad, serrated.

Habit: Vigorous but slightly straggly growth, soon almost trailing with the weight of leaves and flowers. Very free-flowering.

Positioning: Ideal as a bush, both in large pots and planted outdoors in summer in full sun, but needs support to maintain an upright habit; also makes an excellent weeping standard. Almost hardy in many gardens.

Care: Quite undemanding. Main stems can become bare as they develop unless plants are pinched once or twice while still small.

Useful tips: Try growing this in a hanging basket, allowing the stems to bend naturally.

Nellie Nuttall

Type: Single, medium-sized flowers.

Tube: Bright red; medium length and thickness.

Sepals: Bright red; held firmly outwards.

Corolla: Snow white, with slight red veining; facing stiffly outwards.

Foliage: Small, mid green.

Habit: Strong and vigorous, upright stems freely branching to produce a neat bushy plant. Very free-flowering.

Positioning: Plant out in summer in a lightly shaded spot, but does best in a large pot indoors; may also be trained as a spectacular full or half-size standard for indoor display.

Care: Very easy to grow. Plants intended as bushes need pinching several times to induce branching, and regular feeding to stimulate rapid growth.

Useful tips: With their strong straight branches, plants can be trained on a supporting framework as outstanding fans and espaliers.

A fairly modern introduction by George Roe and considered by many to be an improvement on the famous red and white 'Snowcap'. Not as hardy as that old variety, but more prolific, with blooms that tend to be held well out from the foliage.

Orange Drops

One of the very best orange varieties, with elegant and intensely coloured flowers hanging in conspicuous clusters on stems that cannot decide if they are upright, trailing or trying to grow sideways.

Type:	Single, medium-sized flowers.
Tube:	Light orange and waxen; long and of medium thickness.
Sepals:	Light orange with green tips; broad, pointed and horizontal.
Corolla:	Orange with smoked pink edges and darker mottling at the base of petals.
Foliage:	Largish, mid-green.
Habit:	Fairly vigorous and upright at first, but soon declining to horizontal, even trailing positions. Fairly free-flowering.
Positioning:	May be grown in pots and planted outdoors in summer as half-hardy bedding in light shade; also grown in hanging baskets, especially under glass.
Care:	Pinch out early and frequently to shape growth. Some plants trail quite early and should be grown in raised or hanging pots.
Useful tips:	Train young plants on strong supports to form weeping standards for display under glass or outdoors in a sheltered place.

Type: Single, small-flowered.

Tube: White and waxy; medium length, and quite thick.

Sepals: White and waxy, with green tips; narrow, short and held horizontal, with some reflexing.

Corolla: Pink with white shading at base of petals; small and compact.

Foliage: Small, medium green, and finely serrated.

Habit: Vigorous upright growth, with strong stems branching quite freely. Free-flowering.

Positioning: Ideal as pot plants indoors; also suitable outdoors in containers or in open ground as summer bedders.

Care: Undemanding, although careful watering at all stages is important. Pot in free-draining soil-based compost and make sure outdoor plants are not grown in water-logged positions. Pinch to encourage bushy growth.

Useful tips: Train as a full or half standard, a shape that complements the formality of the flowers.

A very fine small-flowered variety, the size of its blooms more than balanced by the strikingly prolific display. Although dainty in their general appearance, plants are robust and suitable for almost any situation.

Pee Wee Rose

A cheerful and energetic variety which can be used in various situations, for it sits mid-way between a trailing fuchsia and a small hardy shrub that makes an attractive edging plant. Small-flowered but prolific, laden with blooms all summer. (syn. 'Peewee Rose'.)

Type: Single, small-flowered.

Tube: Light rosy red; thin, medium length.

Sepals: Light rosy red; longish, held stiffly downwards over the corolla.

Corolla: Rich rosy red; small, very compact and neatly furled.

Foliage: Small, mid-green and serrated.

Habit: Very vigorous and fast-growing, the long branches arching gracefully. Very free-flowering.

Positioning: Best in a hanging basket or in the front of a border where it has room to trail. As a hardy edging plant it will grow to 45cm (18in) high.

Care: Pinch out young plants several times to encourage branching. Plants grown outdoors can be protected with a mulch of leaves in winter; prune stems back half-way in autumn and complete pruning in spring.

Useful tips: This is worth training as a half-standard in a large pot, building up a strong head of arching stems.

Phyllis

Type: Single or semi-double, small to medium-sized flowers.

Tube: Bright rosy red and waxy; short and thick.

Sepals: Bright rosy red and waxy; broad and drooping over the corolla.

Corolla: Deeper rose red; compact.

Foliage: Small to medium-sized, mid-green, serrated.

Habit: Vigorous and fast-growing, quickly making a stiff shrub 90cm (3ft) high and wide. Free-flowering.

Positioning: Difficult to train indoors and too vigorous for all but very large pots, unless trained as a tall standard. Young plants can be grown in borders with plenty of space. Permanent outdoor plants do well in full sun or shade.

Care: Pinch young plants once or twice. Plant out in late spring; repot bedders in autumn to bring indoors or take cuttings and leave parent plants outside.

Useful tips: Train standards in a season in 18–20cm (7–8in) pots.

Sometimes credited with being the best of all hardy fuchsias, this develops rapidly into a large stout shrub that is covered in small bright flowers from early in the season until the first frosts of autumn.

Pink Marshmallow

Very well known, and a favourite large-flowered variety among fuchsia enthusiasts. The buds and blooms can reach an enormous size, while avoiding most of the problems often associated with other large double-flowered kinds.

Type: Double, very large-flowered.

Tube: Very pale pink; quite long, medium thickness.

Sepals: Very pale pink with green tips; broad and reflexing.

Corolla: White, veined pink and with pink shading; elongated and full, creating the impression of a double skirt.

Foliage: Large, light green and serrated.

Habit: Moderately vigorous, producing long flexible stems that branch freely. Free-flowering all season.

Positioning: Perfect for hanging baskets, under glass, or outdoors protected from winds.

Care: Pinch young plants once or twice to encourage early branching, and as trailing growth develops hang pots clear of the staging or plant in baskets to avoid cramping the lateral branches.

Useful tips: Plants flower well outdoors, but blooms are smaller than those produced under glass.

Type: Single, small-flowered.

Tube: White, flushed pink; short and thick.

Sepals: Creamy white, flushed rose pink, with green tips; short, broad and held well out arching over the corolla.

Corolla: Rosy purple, white at base; compact.

Foliage: Small, mid-green and serrated.

Habit: Very vigorous, with flexible stems branching freely to produce a bushy, naturally trailing plant. Very free-flowering.

Positioning: Ideal for hanging baskets, outdoors and under glass; may be trained as a short standard indoors.

Care: Very easy to grow and propagate, and totally trouble free. Pinch young plants once or twice to induce self-branching, and feed regularly during flowering.

Useful tips: Before the first autumn frosts bring hanging baskets into the greenhouse or conservatory where, with a little heat, plants may flower all winter.

A seedling from 'La Campanella', sharing its parent's vigour and high qualities as a basket variety. The attractive blooms are produced over an exceptionally long season outdoors, only frost putting an end to the display.

Powder Puff

The soft delicate colouring of its blooms, especially when highlighted by the bright red of the opening stamens, makes this a great favourite with collectors of double-flowered fuchsias. When fully laden with blooms a well-grown plant looks entrancing.

Type: Double, medium-sized flowers.

Tube: Clear tyrian rose; medium length and thickness.

Sepals: Clear tyrian rose, with a deeper shade on undersides; stiffly recurving.

Corolla: Apple blossom pink; compact and very full.

Foliage: Medium-sized, mid-green with prominent veins.

Habit: Very vigorous, with long arching stems that are flexible and self-branching. Very free-flowering.

Positioning: Looks most effective in hanging baskets in very light shade, outdoors with shelter from wind and rain, or under glass.

Care: Start with early spring cuttings and pinch out each plant whenever growth has made two to three pairs of leaves; do this three times before transferring the young plants to baskets and growing on under glass for a few weeks.

Useful tips: Train a half-standard in an 18cm (7in) pot for display under glass.

Princessita

Type: Single, medium-sized flowers.

Tube: White; slender and medium length.

Sepals: White with a slight pink flush on the underside; long, narrow and gracefully upturned.

Corolla: Very deep rose pink; medium-sized with a slightly open arrangement of petals.

Foliage: Medium-sized, mid- to dark green, serrated.

Habit: Very vigorous with long strong stems that are naturally trailing and branching freely. Free-flowering all season.

Positioning: Perfect for a hanging basket or for flowering under glass, always with a little shade. May be grown in a half-basket on a sheltered wall outdoors; also in a large pot in a greenhouse.

Care: Start early in the season with fresh cuttings, and pinch several times while small for full self-branching.

Useful tips: Train as a half-standard for planting outdoors in summer.

A very fine variety for hanging baskets, with attractive blooms, of classic shape and eye-catching colour, often studding the full length of the arching bushy growth. Reliable and very satisfying in most positions.

Red Spider

A famous American variety with an unattractive name. Plants resemble 'Cascade' in habit and in their ability to hide the dense bushy branches with a quite outstanding number of brilliantly coloured flowers that always give great pleasure.

Type: Single, medium-sized flowers.

Tube: Crimson; long and slender.

Sepals: Crimson; long, narrow and reflexed.

Corolla: Rose madder with deeper shading on the edges of petals; large, neatly overlapping.

Foliage: Small to medium-sized, mid-green, very thick and serrated.

Habit: Extremely vigorous, the long branches growing strongly to form a natural cascade. Very free-flowering.

Positioning: Popular in large baskets for outdoor display or under glass, but also ideal in large pots or containers outdoors and as part of greenhouse displays.

Care: Plants need frequent pinching while small to create a uniform framework of side-shoots. Keep the foliage as dry as possible to avoid mould.

Useful tips: In hot summers check leaves for red spider mite. Plants can be trained to make weeping standards.

Riccartonii

Type: Single, small-flowered.

Tube: Rich scarlet; short and fairly thick.

Sepals: Rich scarlet; long, slim and gently recurved, pointing downwards.

Corolla: Deep purple; short and compact.

Foliage: Small to medium-sized, mid- to dark green with a reddish-bronze tint, rather long.

Habit: Robust and vigorous, the long sturdy stems branching to produce side-shoots that bend almost to the ground under the weight of blooms. Very free-flowering.

Positioning: Not for indoor cultivation. May be grown in tubs outdoors, or in a mixed border.

Care: Undemanding. Watch out for aphids and whitefly during summer and spray with a systemic insecticide. Mulch thickly over winter in cool districts, and cut back all dead stems in mid-spring.

Useful tips: Hardy enough to have naturalized widely in milder areas. Plant 60cm (2ft) apart for an attractive hedge.

A very old variety, introduced in 1833, and probably the hardiest hybrid of the species *Fuchsia magellanica*. A great favourite for informal hedging that looks most appealing when its branches are laden with the long brilliant flowers often called 'lady's eardrops'.

Rose of Castile

Introduced in the mid-nineteenth century and still regarded with affection as an easy variety, often the first that new gardeners grow. Notable for its long flowering season, the bright, almost luminous flowers opening in an unbroken sequence until the first autumn frosts.

Type: Single, small-flowered.

Tube: White and waxy, with a greenish tinge; short, thick and rounded.

Sepals: Waxy white, hint of pink on underside, green tipped; short, pointed, held well out.

Corolla: Reddish-purple, white at base of petals, white streak in centre of each; compact.

Foliage: Small, light or mid-green, finely serrated.

Habit: Extremely vigorous and strong-growing, with stiff upright stems that branch freely. Very free-flowering.

Positioning: Grow in pots under glass or in containers outside during summer; also plant out as specimen shrubs or in summer bedding. May be trained as a strong standard. In mild gardens can be treated as a hardy shrub.

Care: Pinch young plants once or twice to induce self-branching. Give plants grown outdoors a deep protective mulch over winter.

Useful tips: 'Rose of Castile Improved' has larger flowers.

Type: Double, medium-sized flowers.

Tube: White with a green or pale pink flush; short and thick.

Sepals: White to pale pink, deeper pink at base; short, broad, reflexed.

Corolla: White; round, full and flaring.

Foliage: Medium to large, mid-green, neat, shapely.

Habit: Moderately vigorous, with sturdy upright stems that branch freely to form tidy open bushes. Free-flowering.

Positioning: A good bush for pot cultivation indoors or for bedding out in summer in a lightly shaded spot sheltered from winds; may also be grown as a standard indoors, or outside as a 'dot' plant in summer bedding.

Care: Pinch young plants several times while still small. Avoid wetting the flowers and foliage on indoor plants to help prevent mould from developing.

Useful tips: The stiff growth is an ideal basis for training plants into other formal shapes.

A slightly exotic double variety with neat tightly packed flowers borne in clusters at the ends of its branches. Just as attractive before the blooms open, the buds hanging like fat immaculate tear-drops full of promise.

Royal Velvet

One of the best all-round fuchsias, a regal plant with richly coloured blooms that have none of the coarseness associated with many doubles, especially in this colour range. A versatile plant, easily trained into a number of forms, and often seen exhibited.

Type:	Double, medium-sized or large flowers.
Tube:	Shiny crimson; medium length and thickness.
Sepals:	Shiny crimson, underside paler, matt and crêped; short, broad and held out over the corolla.
Corolla:	Deep purple, outer petals splashed crimson at their base; very full and fluffy.
Foliage:	Medium-sized and mid- to deep green, veined red with red stalks, finely serrated.
Habit:	Moderately vigorous, upright at first but later arching under the weight of the blooms. Very free-flowering especially under glass.
Positioning:	Grow in pots under glass or in larger containers outdoors; with pinching it excels as a semi-trailer in window-boxes. Ideal for training as a large standard.
Care:	Plants need frequent pinching while small to make the best self-supporting bushes.
Useful tips:	Cuttings root very easily in autumn or spring.

| ** | 🍓 | 🪴 |

Type: Single, medium-sized flowers.

Tube: Rich bright red; medium length and thickness.

Sepals: Red; fairly long, narrow and recurving.

Corolla: Bright dusky red; long and compact.

Foliage: Medium to large, light to mid-green, slightly serrated, incised veins.

Habit: Very vigorous, with strong upright stems that branch freely. Very free-flowering.

Positioning: A fine weatherproof bush for bedding out in summer; also first-class in a pot under glass or larger containers outdoors. Easily trained as a large standard.

Care: Pinch plants frequently while young to encourage dense bushy growth. Plants are almost hardy, and after full hardening off may be bedded out in late spring.

Useful tips: Restrict the size of pot at first to stimulate early blooms to develop, and then feed regularly to maintain the copious display in autumn.

A very popular variety, so easy to grow that it is often recommended as a beginner's plant, although many exhibitors also depend on its ability to produce neat shapely plants with masses of well displayed flowers. (syn. 'Rufus the Red'.)

Distinctive and memorable in full bloom, a landmark variety that represented a new colour break in fuchsias, with the unusual and lovely markings of its corolla often looking almost hand-painted as it matures. Worth growing for its size and originality.

Type: Single, large-flowered.

Tube: Pale greenish-white; short and rather thick.

Sepals: White with green-flecked tips; medium length, broad and slightly reflexing.

Corolla: Dark red, fading to bright red with streaks of white down centre of each large petal.

Foliage: Medium-sized, pale to mid-green, smooth and rounded.

Habit: Vigorous and sturdy, with thick upright stems branching to make a strong, reasonably bushy plant. Very free-flowering.

Positioning: Best as a bush under glass in a large pot, at least 20cm (8in) diameter, or outdoors in a container in a sheltered spot.

Care: Frequent pinching while plants are young often prevents later leaf loss from lower stems. Very susceptible to mould; keep dry and spray with fungicide at the first signs.

Useful tips: Thin overlapping leaves to improve air circulation and help prevent mould.

Seventh Heaven

Type: Double, large-flowered.

Tube: White; fairly long and thick.

Sepals: White with pink tinge, crêped and upturned at tips.

Corolla: Intense orange-red with white streaks at base; very full and shapely.

Foliage: Large, dark green, red midribs and stalks.

Habit: Strong growth, the stems at first upright but soon arching. Free-flowering, especially at first, and again after a brief rest.

Positioning: A choice basket variety that succeeds outdoors if sheltered from winds; also under glass where flowering is even more prolific. With support may be grown in pots indoors, or outside in summer.

Care: Pinch out young plants early and frequently, and if necessary weight longer branches to coax them into trailing downwards. Feed plants in the pause between flowering.

Useful tips: Train strong cuttings as weeping standards for indoors.

A modern variety from the USA, this is an outstanding fuchsia for hanging baskets, with strong trailing stems and plenty of large double blooms that are remarkable for their depth of colour.

There are many white fuchsias, but this is arguably one of the finest, with interesting contrasts between the greenish-white tube and pinkish-white sepals, and the corolla that may be pure white or creamy ivory according to the season and the amount of sunlight.

Type: Double, medium-sized flowers.

Tube: White, flushed pale pink or greenish-white; long and slender.

Sepals: White with touch of pink at the base and deeper pink underneath; long, broad, slightly reflexed.

Corolla: White or creamy white; fairly full.

Foliage: Medium-sized, rich mid-green, and slightly serrated.

Habit: Very vigorous, the strong stems branching freely to produce a dense plant. Free-flowering all season.

Positioning: Normally grown as a bush, for display under glass in pots or as summer bedding.

Care: Pinch early and regularly. Harden off thoroughly before transferring outdoors after last frosts, to warm positions sheltered from winds. Watch out for mould, and spray with fungicide if necessary.

Useful tips: After one or two early stops, the stiff branches can be trained as a fan for indoor display.

Sleigh Bells

Type: Single, large-flowered.

Tube: Pure white; short and fairly thick.

Sepals: Pure white; very long and narrow with pale green tips. Recurving or horizontal.

Corolla: Pure white; large and inflated like a bell.

Foliage: Medium-sized, mid- to dark green, incised and serrated.

Habit: Moderately vigorous with slender, fairly upright stems that later arch under the weight of blooms. Very free-flowering.

Positioning: Excellent under glass in pots, or planted out in summer, in containers or as bedding in sheltered, light shade. Can be trained as a standard, for pot culture or as a 'dot' plant outdoors.

Care: Pinch out while small. Harden off thoroughly before planting out and rehouse before autumn frosts and rains.

Useful tips: For the best colour avoid wetting the flowers and always shade from bright sunlight.

Another very fine white fuchsia, with quite flamboyant single flowers that are pure dense white when grown in light shade. The full bell-shaped corolla gives blooms plenty of body, balanced by the long graceful sepals that extend far out to the sides. Very satisfying when well grown.

Snowcap

Indispensable to all fuchsia enthusiasts and constantly listed among the top favourites. A very good-tempered variety that withstands training or neglect, and always manages to produce a prolific display of flowers.

Type: Semi-double, small to medium-sized flowers.

Tube: Bright scarlet; short and fairly thick.

Sepals: Bright scarlet; short, broad, held well out.

Corolla: White, veined with cerise especially at the base of petals; rather loose but shapely.

Foliage: Small, mid- to dark green, serrated.

Habit: Vigorous and strong-growing, producing sturdy shoots that branch freely. Very free-flowering.

Positioning: Bushes are easily trained for growing in pots, indoors or outside; also make effective summer bedding. Good standards, pyramids and espaliers are easy to grow.

Care: Simple to grow and to propagate. Pinch young plants early and often. Feed larger plants regularly to sustain the heavy flowering.

Useful tips: In mild gardens the variety is virtually hardy and is worth planting permanently in a sheltered position.

Type: Double, medium- to large-flowered.

Tube: Pale pink; short and fairly thick.

Sepals: Pale pink; lighter towards tip and with green tips; very long, broad and held slightly below the horizontal.

Corolla: Creamy white; very full and compact, the petals almost swirling.

Foliage: Small to medium-sized, mid-green with red midribs and veins.

Habit: Moderately vigorous, with rather long stems that form a bushy, semi-trailing plant. Very free-flowering.

Positioning: Quite good for baskets, but often more effective in a half-basket on a wall; may be grown as a bush with some support, in pots indoors or containers outside.

Care: Pinch plants early and frequently for a satisfactory shape. Cool airy surroundings encourage flowering; buds may fail to open in warm, dry conditions.

Useful tips: Grow in a basket in a cool shaded porch.

As its name implies this is a beautiful and sophisticated variety, with extravagant flowers in rather refined shades of pink, and also with a reputation for being slightly difficult unless its precise needs are indulged.

Swingtime

Generally considered to be the best red and white fuchsia, this is quite hardy but a difficult shape to maintain permanently outdoors. It is ideal for every other purpose, however, and remains one of the great favourites of all time.

Type: Double, large-flowered.

Tube: Shiny scarlet; fairly short and thick.

Sepals: Shiny scarlet above, rose red underneath and crêped; broad and reflexing.

Corolla: Milky white with scarlet veining towards the base of petals; very full and folded.

Foliage: Medium-sized, mid- to darkish green with red midrib and veins.

Habit: Extremely vigorous, upright at first but the stems soon arching and branching freely. Very free-flowering.

Positioning: Good for baskets, indoors or out; if supported can be grown as a bush for pots or for summer bedding in full sun or light shade, with some shelter. Easily trained as standard, espalier or pyramids.

Care: Bushes need early and frequent pinching and support. To trail fully, train main side-shoots down with weights.

Useful tips: A standard can be made quickly and will last years if pruned annually.

Tennessee Waltz

Type: Semi-double, medium-sized flowers.

Tube: Light red; medium length and thickness.

Sepals: Light red; long, broad and curving upwards towards the tube.

Corolla: Lilac-lavender, with splashes of rose; large and fairly loose with uneven petal length.

Foliage: Medium-sized, mid-green, slightly serrated.

Habit: Very vigorous, upright growth. Very free-flowering.

Positioning: Plants succeed in pots indoors or containers in the garden; also as summer bedding in sun or shade. Very hardy and may be grown permanently outside in a warm sheltered site. Easily trained as a standard for indoor display or as a 'dot' plant outdoors in summer.

Care: Pinch young plants to make the fullest bushes. Plants grown outdoors need well-prepared sites and protection over winter.

Useful tips: May also be grown as a pillar or pyramid.

A graceful and colourful semi-double variety that can be recommended to any beginner for its ease of cultivation and the rapid and spectacular results that may be achieved in a short time. Outstanding for both home and exhibition use.

Thalia

Best known of all the *Fuchsia triphylla* hybrids, very popular for its lush opulent foliage and proud upright habit. The strong branches end in huge terminal clusters of slender, vividly coloured flowers at their best late in the season.

Type: Single, very long *triphylla* flowers.

Tube: Rich flame red; long and very slender.

Sepals: Flame red; very small and pointed.

Corolla: Orange-scarlet; short and compact.

Foliage: Dark olive green, with magenta veins and ribs, and a metallic lustre, tapering to a point.

Habit: Very robust and vigorous, with tall stout stems, almost upright but branching to form well-shaped bushes. Very free-flowering.

Positioning: Spectacular grown in large pots for display under glass; may also be planted out as 'dot' plants among summer bedding or as shrubs in warm sheltered sites with full sun.

Care: Pinch young plants frequently. Feed every fortnight and do not expose to low temperatures. Bring indoors before first frosts, and overwinter at 10°C (50°F).

Useful tips: Try planting out in a large tub for the summer.

Type:	Single, medium-sized flowers.
Tube:	White; fairly long and thick.
Sepals:	White with green tips; long, narrow and curling upwards.
Corolla:	White with a trace of pink at the base of petals; widely open and bell shaped.
Foliage:	Medium-sized, light or mid-green and smooth, with serrated edges.
Habit:	Very vigorous and strong-growing, producing stout upright stems. Free-flowering.
Positioning:	Grown under glass because of the flowers' sensitivity to light and weather. May be bushes or standards for pots; also grown in containers outdoors in summer with shelter from sun and rain.
Care:	Pinch young plants early and often. Wetting the flowers marks the petals. The foliage is susceptible to mould so take care not to wet the leaves either; ventilate freely.
Useful tips:	In a damp year routine sprays of fungicide deter against mould.

A rewarding variety to grow well, when the plants are decked with huge numbers of intensely white bells, each of them packed with clear pink stamens. Excellent as an all-round fuchsia for the greenhouse, where the blooms are safe from the weather.

The best hanging basket varieties are brightly coloured and prolific: this would be the perfect choice, for the vivid flowers are produced in huge numbers over the full summer season with complete reliability.

Type:	Double, medium-sized flowers.
Tube:	Crimson; long and very slender.
Sepals:	Crimson; long, narrow and reflexed.
Corolla:	Rosy purple, slightly paler at base of petals; compact and well furled.
Foliage:	Medium-sized, mid-green and serrated.
Habit:	Very vigorous growth, with strong stems that form bushy trailing plant. Very free-flowering.
Positioning:	A perfect basket plant, flowering well under glass and outdoors in full sun. With careful staking half-standards and pyramids are easily trained under glass in pots.
Care:	Easy to grow and propagate. Start early in the season with fresh cuttings, and pinch out to make a well-branched plant.
Useful tips:	With careful training strong cuttings can be shaped into weeping standards, but these will take two to three seasons to build up dense heads.

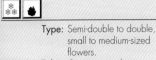

Type: Semi-double to double, small to medium-sized flowers.

Tube: Carmine; medium length and thickness.

Sepals: Carmine; short, broad and upturned.

Corolla: White, veined with carmine and with a carmine flush at the base of petals; fairly full and compact.

Foliage: Small, mid-green, finely serrated.

Habit: Vigorous upright growth, with strong stems arching under the weight of blooms. Very free-flowering.

Positioning: Ideal for pots indoors under glass and containers outdoors; also for bedding or edging to beds and borders. Plants can be grown permanently, in full sun or light shade.

Care: Pinch young plants a couple of times while small. Plant out in late spring after hardening off; mulch over winter. Prune dead stems in spring.

Useful tips: Plants may be grown 30cm (12in) apart as permanent seasonal edging.

Reliably hardy fuchsias are valuable assets in the garden, especially when they can also be grown as specimen plants under glass. This is a tough and versatile variety, with bright cheerful flowers and a notably easy-going constitution.

Wave of Life

A long-established foliage plant, well over a century old, and still highly regarded for its brightly coloured leaves. As with all coloured forms, the blooms are a bonus and do not appear in prolific numbers, although they make strong highlights against the gold background.

Type: Single, small-flowered.

Tube: Scarlet; slim and fairly long.

Sepals: Scarlet with greenish-white tips; short, broad and upturned.

Corolla: Reddish-purple; small, compact, neatly furled.

Foliage: Small to medium-sized, greenish-yellow and gold, serrated with pink stems.

Habit: Moderately vigorous, the slender stems soon arching over to form a fairly well-branched bush. Small numbers of flowers are produced late in the season.

Positioning: Grown as a pot plant in a sunny greenhouse or conservatory; can be planted outdoors in summer as edging and coloured groups with bedding plants. Also suitable for hanging baskets in full sun.

Care: Pinch young plants several times especially if trailing plants are required, and feed regularly. Always grow in full sun to maintain good colour.

Useful tips: Plant several specimens in a single basket for full impact.